INSPIRATIONAL ANIMALS COLORING BOOK

This book belongs to:

____

DON'T STOP.
GALLOP TO A BRIGHTER DAY

THERE'S A ROOM
FOR TWO IN MY
SHELL

STRETCH
YOUR
IMAGINATION

FEELING LOW?
LET ME PICK
YOU UP!

SCARED?
TAKE MY PAW

A SONG IS BETTER SUNG TOGETHER

TIMES are HARD
NEED a BEAR HUG?

LIKE a RAINSTORM
THIS also
WILL PASS

WE CAN WADDLE
THIS STORM
TOGETHER

FLY WITH ME
to a better
TOMORROW

Chase
Your Dreams

BE a DREAMER
and
NEVER GIVE UP

FIN UP
TOMORROW WILL BE BETTER

TREAT
every day
LIKE an
ACCOMPLISHMENT

WE WILL BE STRONG

EMBRACE
HOPE

IT'S YOUR FUTURE
DREAM BIG!

HOP
TOWARD
YOUR DREAMS

HOLD ON
to
HOPE

REGROUP,
THEN CONQUER

MY LEAF HAS A ROOM FOR ANOTHER

YOU'RE
NOT ALONE
AMONGST
THIS HERD

Leap
EVEN IF THE FUTURE
IS UNCERTAIN

YOU ARE UNIQUELY
you

Made in the USA
Coppell, TX
07 November 2021

65346585R00031